The My Encyclopedia Collection

My Encyclopedia of Baby Animals

My Encyclopedia of the Forest

My Encyclopedia of Insects and Bugs

My Encyclopedia of the Sea

Library of Congress Cataloging-in-Publication Data

Names: Brin, Antoine, author. | Valladares, Lionel, author. | Rawson, Gay, translator.
Title: My encyclopedia of insects and bugs / Antoine Brin and Lionel Valladares ; translated by Gay Rawson, Ph.D.
Description: New York, NY : Children's Press, an Imprint of Scholastic,Inc., [2017] | Series: My encyclopedia |
Translation of an unidentified work. | Includes index.
Identifiers: LCCN 2016008819| ISBN 9780531224700 (library binding) | ISBN 9780531225943 (hardcover)
Subjects: LCSH: Insects–Juvenile literature. | Insects–Encyclopedias, Juvenile.
Classification: LCC QL467.2 .B75 2017 | DDC 595.7–dc23 LC record available at http://lccn.loc.gov/2016008819

Produced by Spooky Cheetah Press
Translation by Gay Rawson

Mon encyclo des petites bêtes © Éditions Milan 2010
Translation © 2017 Scholastic Inc.

Printed in China 62

My encyclOpedia of insects and bugs

Antoine Brin
Lionel Valladares

Table of Contents

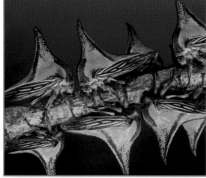

Creepy Crawly

Welcome to the universe of insects, bugs, and more! You can see them every day: on the ground, in the air, on flowers, and even in your house.

Insects

Like other little bugs, insects do not have bones.
They are invertebrates. They have an external skeleton.

Ground Beetles

An insect's body is divided into three parts that you can easily see on the ground beetle: a head, a thorax, and an abdomen. Some beetles are nocturnal. Others are active both during the day and at night.

There are many types of beetles. Some are very fancy.

Grasshoppers

Like all insects, the grasshopper has two antennae, six legs, and four wings. Grasshoppers eat a variety of grasses and plants.

The grasshopper usually uses its large legs to jump away from danger, but it can also fly.

The dragonfly lives near ponds, rivers, and streams. It is great at hunting small insects.

Dragonflies

Dragonflies have excellent vision thanks to their large compound eyes. A dragonfly's eyes cover almost its entire head, giving the insect almost 360° vision.

Butterflies

The butterfly has two pairs of clearly visible wings. They have many different colors and designs depending on the species. This pretty insect has long antennae on its head.

This is a brimstone butterfly. Brimstones are easy to spot in spring.

Arachnids

A spider is not an insect. It is an arachnid.
A spider has eight legs and its body is
divided into two parts instead of three.

Black Widows

Careful! The black widow is a
very venomous species that can
be dangerous. The black widow
rarely attacks people, though.
Insects are its usual prey!

You can recognize the
black widow by the red
hourglass shape on its
otherwise all-black abdomen.

Wolf Spiders

The wolf spider got its name from the way
it hunts. Many species chase down their
prey before killing it with a bite. If it sits
on the ground without moving, you could
walk right past a wolf spider without even
seeing it. It's well camoflauged.

Like most spiders, the
wolf spider has eight
simple eyes with no facets.

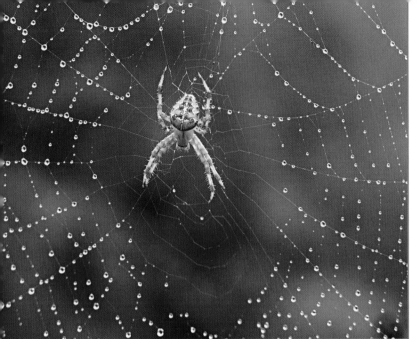

Look at the garden spider's beautiful web. Its strands are made of silk.

Garden Spiders

The garden spider weaves a beautiful web to catch insects in flight. Once an insect gets stuck in the web, it is trapped. The spider then kills its prey and eats it.

Crab Spiders

A crab spider's two front legs are much bigger than the others. They usually hold them open, so they can grab their prey. That's where this spider got its name.

The crab spider often uses ambush to catch prey, such as this bee.

Jumping Spiders

This amazing arachnid can leap more than 30 times its own length! Before it leaps, the jumping spider attaches a bit of web, called a dragline, to the spot from which it is launching. That acts as a safety line.

The jumping spider leaps on its prey.

Arthropods

Scorpions and other small invertebrates are part of the arachnid group. Like spiders, they have four pairs of legs and simple eyes. They do not have wings or antennae.

Scorpions

One way a scorpion differs from a spider is that it has one pair of big pincers. It also has an abdomen that ends in a small kind of spine called a stinger.

The scorpion uses its stinger to inject paralyzing venom into its prey.

Tailless Whip Scorpions

Also called the amblypygi, this scorpion lives in warm, humid regions. During the day, it hides under loose bark or in hollow trees or logs. At night it hunts insects, spiders, and moths.

The tailless whip scorpion's legs are very long and slender.

The pseudoscorpion lives under tree bark and dead leaves.

False Scorpions

The pseudoscorpion, also called a false scorpion, is less than half an inch long. It looks like a scorpion without a tail. The pseudoscorpion eats parasites.

Daddy Longlegs

You can recognize the daddy longlegs by its delicate and very long legs. Its slender legs break off very easily, so you may see daddy longlegs with fewer than eight legs!

Daddy longlegs are not dangerous.

Crustaceans

All crustaceans have a hard outer skeleton called an exoskeleton. They also have two pairs of antennae.

Crayfish

The crayfish is a freshwater crustacean. It has two large pincers that make it look like a mini lobster.

The crayfish moves around on its five pairs of legs.

Woodlice

Most crustaceans live in the water but the woodlouse lives on the ground, often in humid and dark places. It eats dead leaves.

The woodlouse has an articulated shell, which means it can roll itself into a ball when it senses danger.

This tadpole shrimp might look strange. In some parts of the world, people think its shell looks like a shield!

Tadpole Shrimp

The tadpole shrimp, also called triops, has three eyes. It lives in ponds. It's a living fossil! It has not evolved, or changed, since the age of the dinosaurs.

Freshwater Shrimp

The freshwater shrimp is also called a side swimmer. It swims in the deep parts of waterways and moves by swimming on its side. People sell them dried to feed goldfish.

When the current is strong, freshwater shrimp take shelter among the vegetation.

Millipedes

People call these creatures thousand-leggers, but that is an exaggeration. Even the largest millipedes have fewer than 100 legs.

Striped Millipedes

The striped millipede looks like an earthworm but it has many tiny legs. As it gets older, its body gets longer. So if you are comparing two striped millipedes, you can easily tell which one is older. The longer one!

The striped millipede rolls into a tight coil when it is threatened.

Scolopendra

The scolopendra uses its fangs to kill small bugs and eat them. Some species can be very large.

During the day, the scolopendra hides under rocks or bark.

House Centipedes

You might see a house centipede in your home. It comes out at night to hunt insects. The centipede uses its venom-filled fangs to paralyze its prey before eating it.

The house centipede's long legs help it run fast.

Mollusks

A mollusk doesn't have legs. But the muscular lower part of its body is known as a foot. Mollusks slide across hard surfaces. If they live in water they swim or float along on the current.

Great Pond Snails

The great pond snail is found in ponds, lakes, and marshes. It is a scavenger, feeding mostly on plants, but also on dead animal matter.

The great pond snail has a very pretty spiral-shaped shell.

The Burgundy Snail

This snail has four long, flexible tentacles. The snail's eyes are at the end of the two largest top tentacles. Its lower tentacles contain the snail's smell sensors.

Burgundy snails are a delicacy in France.

Slugs may be gray, brown, yellow—even red.

Slugs

Slugs are basically snails without shells. Like snails, they leave a trail of slime as they move over the ground. Often found in gardens, slugs like to eat plant leaves, fruits, and vegetables.

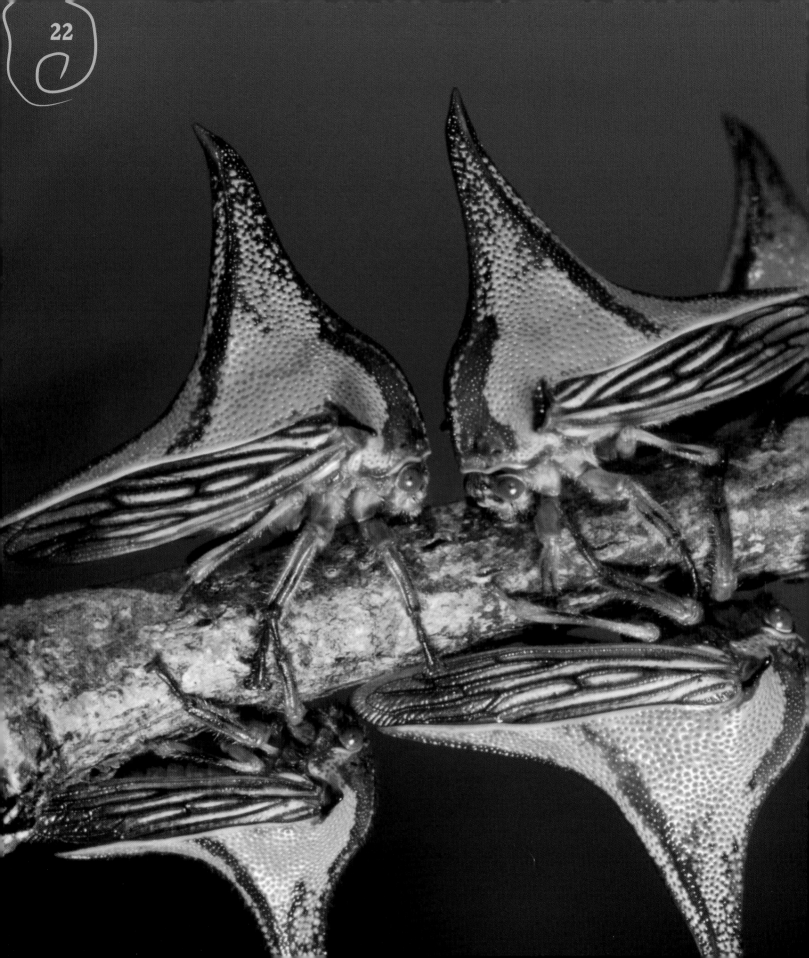

Good Looks

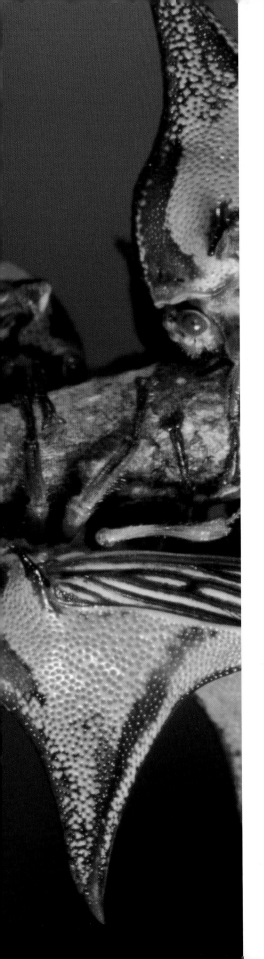

Insects and other little bugs come in a wide variety of shapes and colors. They sometimes look like they are wearing Halloween costumes!

Beautiful Wings

An insect's wings are sometimes hidden when it is not flying. When open, the wings' beautiful colors and splendid designs are revealed.

Transparent Wings

Only adult mayflies have wings. They are almost completely transparent. You can see only some darker lines—the veins. They make the wings stronger.

When not flying, the mayfly keeps its wings folded up, one against the other, on top of its body.

Colorful Wings

Some insects have very bright, colorful wings. The colors may act as camouflage. Or they may warn predators that the insect is toxic.

When the blue-winged grasshopper flies, it looks like a dancer.

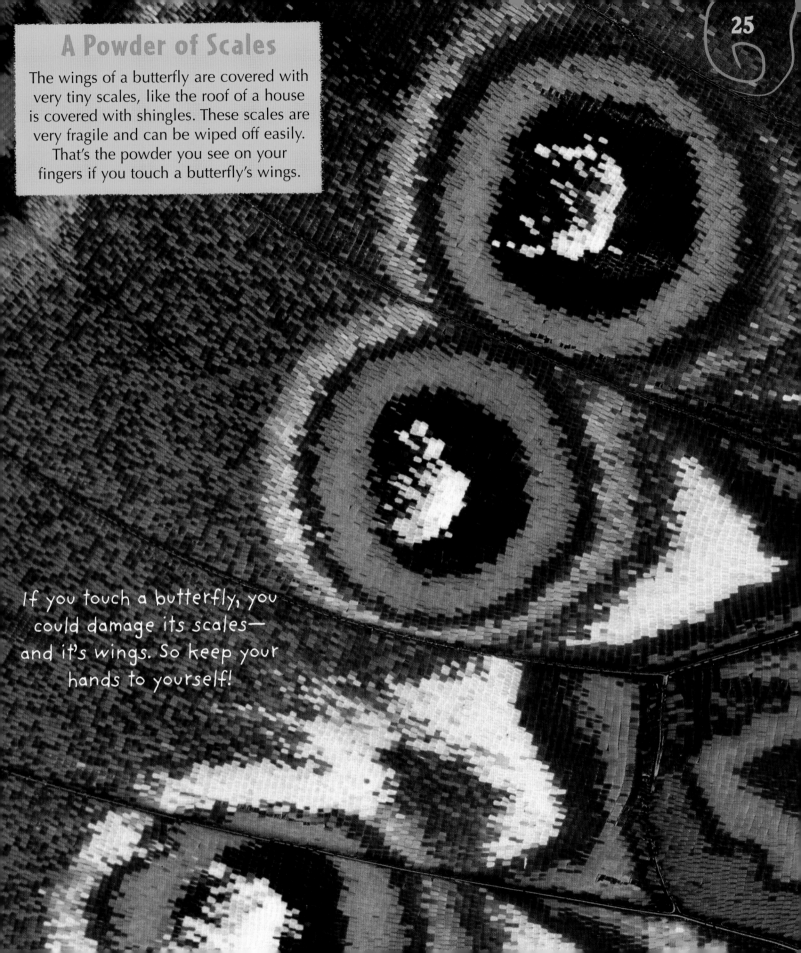

A Powder of Scales

The wings of a butterfly are covered with very tiny scales, like the roof of a house is covered with shingles. These scales are very fragile and can be wiped off easily. That's the powder you see on your fingers if you touch a butterfly's wings.

If you touch a butterfly, you could damage its scales— and it's wings. So keep your hands to yourself!

Many Colors

An insect may have a colorful head, wings, or body.
These colors are good for hiding—and for self-defense.

Love that Sparkle!

Certain insects have a body with a spectacular metallic shine. These colors are a result of the sun's reflection. So they can change depending on the way that you're looking at the insect.

The ruby-tailed wasp was named for its intense and brilliant colors.

Multicolored

The entire palette of colors exists in the insect world. These colors are often helpful in repelling enemies. For example, the monarch butterfly's colors warn birds that it is not good to eat.

The monarch butterfly is recognizable by the intense orange and black colors of its wings.

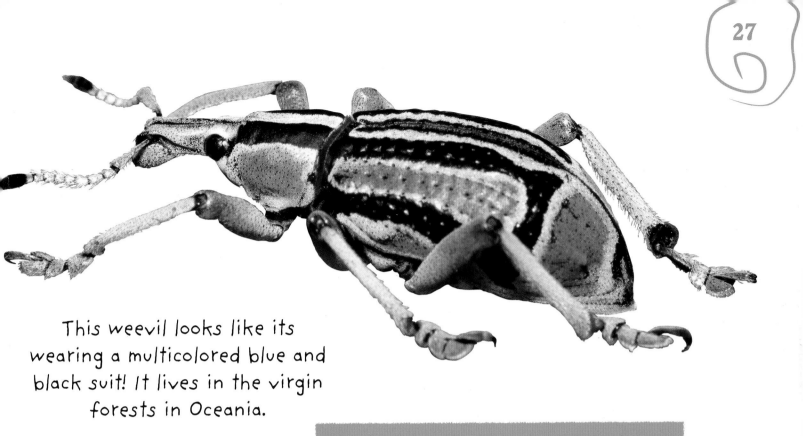

This weevil looks like its wearing a multicolored blue and black suit! It lives in the virgin forests in Oceania.

Stripes

Thanks to its beautiful colored stripes, you can easily spot this weevil among the trees. Scientists wonder what the point of this "make-up" is. Some species have not yet revealed their secrets…

Like a Jewel

For a very long time, humans have been fascinated by the multicolored brilliance of the metallic woodborer. They often used insects like this one to make brooches, earrings, and necklaces.

The metallic woodborer is so beautiful that it has been nicknamed the jeweled beetle.

Surprising Textures

If you touch a variety of insects, you will feel lots of different textures. Their bodies can be soft or hard, hairless or bristly, smooth or rough, dry or slimy...

A Solid Shield

Coleoptera, or beetles, have a hard exoskeleton that covers most of their bodies. They have two pairs of wings. The two front wings are the elytra. The elytra are hard and cover the hind wings. During flight, the beetle holds its elytra out to the sides.

Coleoptera are recognizable by their hard shell.

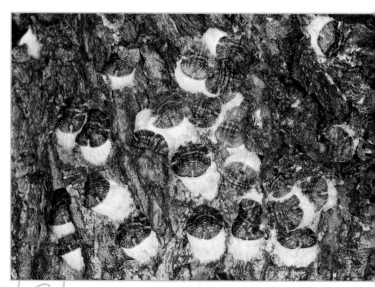

Mealybugs attach themselves to a plant and suck out its juices.

Covered in Cotton

The fleecy mealybug is a small insect that is covered in a white, powdery coating. Mealybugs live in groups. When the colony takes over a plant, it looks like the plant is covered in tiny pieces of cotton.

The black-and-yellow hornet mimic hoverfly looks like a hornet—but it is actually harmless.

A Beautiful Fur Coat

Bees and some flies have a fur coat that often gets covered with dirt or pollen. So it has to be regularly cleaned. Some insects use their bristly legs to comb out the dirt.

A Completely Soft Body

The body of a slug can expand or retract because it is supple. If you pick up a slug, your hands might get covered in slime. A slug secrets mucus that allows it to glide along.

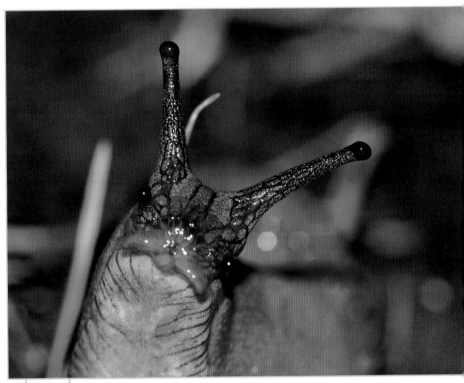

This slug has brilliant soft skin.

In Good Shape!

Insects display many strange shapes. They may be round, flat, or pointed... Some are very unique.

Totally Pointed

Many insects have an elongated, a tapered, or a sharply pointed body. The walking stick looks like a thin branch. The buffalo treehopper mimics the shape of a thorn on a rose bush.

The buffalo treehopper is related to the cicada. Its stocky thorax looks like a buffalo's head!

Totally Round

A lot of insects, like the ladybug for example, have a round shape. A ladybug can fold up its legs and tuck its head under its shell in case of danger.

The green tortoise beetle has a round flat shell. Its two antennae are the only things you see sticking out of it.

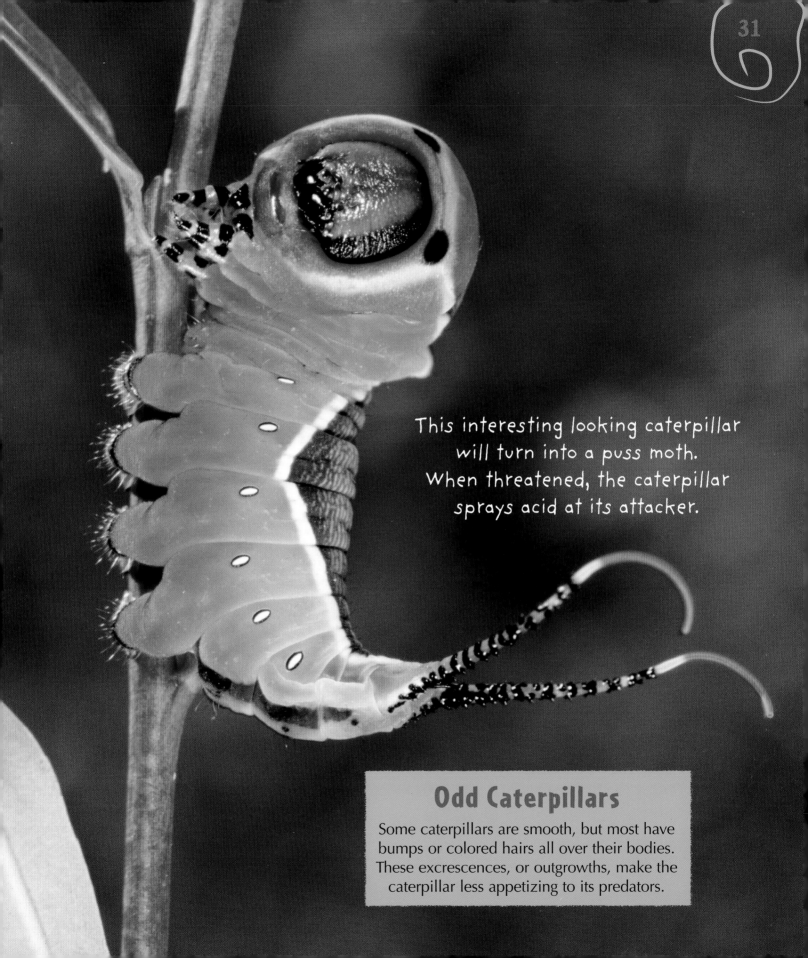

This interesting looking caterpillar will turn into a puss moth. When threatened, the caterpillar sprays acid at its attacker.

Odd Caterpillars

Some caterpillars are smooth, but most have bumps or colored hairs all over their bodies. These excrescences, or outgrowths, make the caterpillar less appetizing to its predators.

Funny Mouths

Different insects have differently shaped mouthparts. But they all have one thing in common—an insect's mouth is very different from your own!

Multiform Mouths

An insect's mouth is made up of several parts whose shapes vary greatly. The mandibles are the first set of jaws. Some insects use them to capture small bugs and cut them up so that the insect can eat them. Mandibles can also be used to carry things. Other insects, like butterflies and bees, have tube-like mouthparts.

Butterflies eat using a proboscis, which is a tube that is used to suck up nectar. When the butterfly isn't eating, the proboscis is coiled up under its head.

A bee's eating mouthpart is the labium. It is used to suck up nectar from flowers.

The male stag beetle has enormous mandibles! He uses them to fight for mates.

ReCOrd HOlders

Incredible strength, a giant or miniscule size, unexpected behavior—these creatures will amaze and surprise you!

The Smallest

To see these critters, you often have to look very closely.
Some are even invisible to the naked eye!

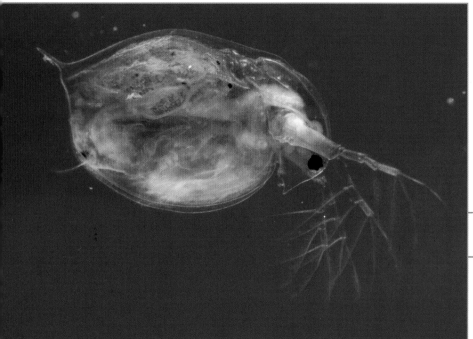

Water Fleas

The daphnia, nicknamed the water flea, is a strange little crustacean that is not even a quarter of an inch (6 millimeters) big. The daphnia lives in freshwater and is often used as food for fish living in aquariums.

The daphnia's nickname comes from the jerky way it swims through the water.

Mites

A member of the same group as spiders, the mite is found everywhere: on certain cheeses, on plant leaves, in the carpet—even on our bodies! They live in colonies.

Some mites are microscopic. The mite in this image has been enlarged 100 times!

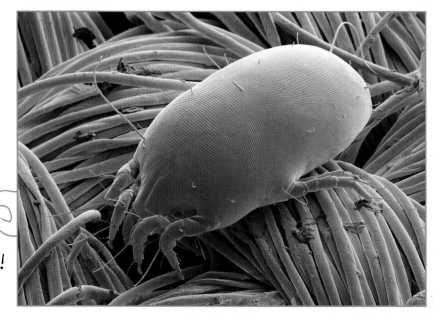

Springtails

The biggest of the springtails is not even a quarter of an inch (6 millimeters) in size. But they are one of the most common insects on earth. If they find a good habitat, millions of these little critters can be found in 2.5 acres (1 hectare) of land.

Springtails don't have wings, so they can't fly. But they can jump.

The Biggest

These little guys are not so little! If you want to meet the biggest of them, you will have to travel— many are found in very remote areas.

Queen Alexandra's Birdwing

The Queen Alexandra's Birdwing is the biggest butterfly ever found. It lives in the tropical rainforests of Papua, New Guinea. This amazing insect is under threat because palm oil plantations are taking over its habitat.

The female Queen Alexandra's Birdwing can have a wingspan of up to 1 foot (31 centimeters).

Giant African Snails

The giant African snail used to be found only in East Africa. Today, however, it can be found all over the world. Unfortunately, this snail is not a welcome guest! It is considered a pest because it devours gardens and crops.

This massive snail can grow to up to 8 inches (20 centimeters).

Poor Knights Wetas

The female Poor Knights weta can reach a length of 8 inches (20 centimeters). That's including its legs and antennae. The weta comes out at night to eat leaves, fruit, and seeds.

The Poor Knight's weta lives in New Zealand.

Titan Beetles

The titan beetle can grow to over 6 inches (15 centimeters) long… not counting its antennae. It is the largest beetle in the Amazon rainforest and has mandibles that can snap a pencil in half!

The titan beetle is almost as large as an adult's hand!

Goliath Birdeaters

The goliath is the largest spider in the world. Its leg span can reach up to 1 foot (30 centimeters). It doesn't really eat birds—though it could if it wanted to! It mainly eats earthworms, insects, frogs, and even rodents.

The Goliath birdeater will attack any prey it comes across. It lives in the Amazon forest.

Spectacular!

Despite their tiny size, some insects have amazing strength. Others move with incredible speed. These are the champions!

Queen of the Air

The fastest insect in the world is the Australian dragonfly. It can fly faster than you can pedal on your bike—up to 35 miles per hour (56 kilometers per hour).

The dragonfly is a true aerial acrobat—it can fly backward and change directions quickly!

A Flea's Jump

Would you believe that a tiny flea is capable of jumping 50 to 100 times its own body length? That would be like you jumping the length of more than two football fields!

At the smallest sign of danger, the flea (seen here under a microscope) leaps incredible distances.

The Hercules beetle lives in the rainforests of Central and South America.

An Efficient Pincer

The male Hercules beetle can grow up to 6.75 inches (17 centimeters) long. It is armed with two long horns that often grow even longer than its body! Males use their horns to fight over females.

Moving Mountains

Dung beetles don't just play in poop—they eat it and lay their eggs in it, too! Some of these creatures can move a ball of dung that weighs 50 times more than they do. Spurs on their back legs help the beetles get the ball rolling.

The beetle moves a huge ball of dung to its hole to feed its grubs.

Strange Lives

An insect's life involves a lot of changes.
The insect starts out as a larva and then transforms
into an adult through a process called metamorphosis.

A Double Life

The grass grub lives two very different lives.
The larva stays underground for about a year and
eats the roots of different plants. The adult lives
outdoors in the fresh air and eats tree leaves.

The grass grub larva looks like a
fat white worm. It's hard to imagine it
will become a beautiful winged adult!

This beetle's elytra don't
cover its large abdomen.

Off on an Adventure

Some blister beetle larvae attach
themselves to adult bees. They travel
to the bees' nest where they feed on
immature bees and stored food.
Adult blister beetles eat the leaves
and flowers of most plants.

The periodical cicada is the longest-lived insect in North America.

A Long Childhood

The periodical cicada spends a long time in the ground as a larva: between 13 and 17 years! The adults come above ground all at the same time, by the thousands, to reproduce.

A Short Life

An adult mayfly has a very brief life— between two minutes and two days. During that time, it doesn't eat. The mayfly's only purpose is to reproduce.

Mayflies lay their eggs in the water. Their larvae can live for up to three years.

Master Migrators

Just like certain kinds of birds, many species of butterfly migrate. They are capable of covering great distances to reproduce or to spend the winter someplace warm.

On the Move

Butterflies migrate for a variety of reasons. They are cold-blooded, so those who live in cool climates travel south in the winter. Other butterflies migrate to start new colonies. In this way, they avoid depleting the food source in their area.

The painted lady butterfly makes a round-trip journey of 9,000 miles (14,500 kilometers) from Africa to the Arctic Circle. No individual lives long enough to make the trip. It takes six generations to complete it.

The death's head hawk moth lives in southern Europe, Africa, and the Middle East. It regularly migrates to northern Europe and Britain.

The monarch is celebrated for its massive and spectacular migrations. As winter approaches, millions of butterflies leave North America headed for warmer weather in Mexico.

Birth and Growth

Whether it lasts a few days or several years, an insect's life has several stages. And different insects have different ways of reproducing.

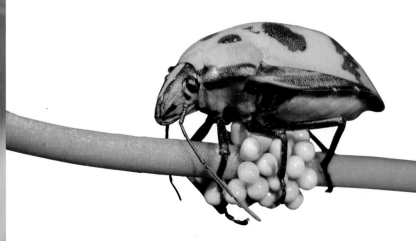

Reproduction

Females usually produce eggs and males usually produce sperm. Both are needed for reproduction. An egg must be fertilized by sperm in order to create a new life.

Mating

If you happen to see two insects that look like they are joined together, they are probably mating. In some cases, the male holds onto the female's back. Some insects, like the dragonfly, can even mate while they are flying!

Coupling allows us to see differences in size, shape, or color between a male and female. This is called sexual dimorphism.

From a Distance

Fertilization does not always require a meeting between a male and female. Bivalve mollusks, like oysters, let their eggs and sperm go loose in the water. Fertilization of the eggs by the sperm is at the mercy of the currents.

The zebra mussel opens his shell to send his sperm into the water.

Mom and Dad

Some creatures, such as earthworms and most snails, have both male and female reproductive organs. They are hermaphrodites. But there still needs to be a coupling in order for babies to be born.

After mating, each of these snails will give birth.

A Slobbery Kiss

Some slugs are true acrobats. When they mate, they interlace and remain suspended in the air by a thick stream of slime. The joining usually takes place at night.

To mate, slugs exchange slime containing sperm. It comes out of a hole on the sides of their heads.

No Daddy!

In some species, an unfertilized egg can still develop into a baby. This phenomenon, called parthenogenesis, allows the female to save energy. She does not have to look for a mate. It's an effective strategy for reproducing quickly!

The female walking stick can give birth to female larvae without the help of any male.

Birth

Whether it is laid in the open air or hidden, or alone or in a group, the egg is the first stage of life for an insect. This stage can last a few days or several months.

A Strange Cradle

Plants where certain small wasps lay their eggs react strangely. They develop an excrescence or gall, whose shape and color vary depending on the type of insect that laid the eggs. Each gall can contain one or several larvae.

The gall on a rose bush hides the larvae. If you see a small hole, that means an insect has already come out!

In a Cocoon

A spider's silk is useful for more than just building webs. The silk can also be used to make a solid cocoon to shelter and transport the spider's eggs. One single cocoon can contain several dozen eggs.

If you see a spider with a little white ball attached to its abdomen, it's a female carrying her cocoon!

The eggs of the green lacewing are easy to recognize. Each is attached to a slender filament called a stalk.

Suspended Eggs

The female green lacewing lays her eggs on white stalks that hang from the bottom of leaves. Her larvae, sometimes called aphid lions, eat a variety of small insects as they grow. Sometimes they even eat each other!

In the Open Air

Many butterflies lay their eggs on the leaves or stems of carefully chosen plants. This will supply the first food for their caterpillars. Even though they are tiny, the eggs are visible and often very colorful.

The praying mantis's eggs are hidden inside a special package called an egg case.

These true bug's eggs measure less than .08 inches (2 millimeters) each.

A Group of Eggs

The praying mantis places all of her eggs in an egg case. This case protects the eggs against bad weather and allows them to spend the winter well sheltered.

Parenting

After hatching, some young larvae have to survive on their own, while others have the help of their parents.

Closely Protected

Whether it is to feed the larvae or to defend them from the male's appetite, some female insects and bugs stays close to their young. This is the case with the common earwig and certain kinds of true bugs who are never far from their young larvae during the first days of their lives.

The female common earwig takes care of her eggs by cleaning them every day. After they hatch, she carefully watches over her babies.

Public Transportation

With scorpions and some kinds of spiders, the female protects her young during the first days of their lives. She can transport several dozen of them on her back at one time.

Perched on their mother's back, these young scorpions fear no predator!

Transferring Custody

The female cuckoo bee lays her eggs in another bee's nest and leaves them there. The bee whose nest it is does not notice the intruders and will take care of them as if they were her own.

The female cuckoo bee acts like the bird with the same name.

Growing Up

Most insects go through metamorphosis.
They grow up in stages before transforming into adults.

Making a New Skin

Crustaceans, certain insects, spiders, and scorpions have a rigid outer cover called an exoskeleton. This prevents them from growing gradually like you. They shed their exoskeleton several times during the growth process. This is called molting.

After an insect molts, a transparent outer skin, called an exuvia, is left behind. You might find one hanging from a plant.

Incomplete Metamorphosis

An insect or arachnid that goes through incomplete metamorphosis has a lifecycle made up of three stages: egg, nymph, and adult. The nymph looks just like the adult, only smaller.

Young spiders are just like adults, only smaller!

The lesser stag beetle starts out as a larva. Then it becomes an immobile pupa, and, finally, an adult.

Complete Metamorphosis

Complete metamorphosis is a lifecycle that has four stages: egg, larva, pupa, and adult. The larvae of butterflies, coleoptera, and flies, for example, are much different than their adult versions. Their growth ends with a profound transformation.

Permanent Growth

Snails are born with very thin, weak shells. The shell will grow continually throughout the snail's entire life. Delicate layers are added, one after the other. That's what makes lines on the shell. The shell becomes thicker and thicker as it grows.

A snail's growth never stops, but it does slow down after the age of 5.

A Butterfly's Life

A butterfly's larva is a caterpillar. It moves by crawling and eats leaves. As an adult, it will be capable of flying and will drink nectar from flowers.

Metamorphosis

Almost entirely black at birth, the small tortoiseshell caterpillar is extremely tiny. It eats nettle leaves and grows to almost an inch (2.54 centimeters) in length. Its body is covered with four yellow-green bands. Then it shuts itself into a cocoon, called a chrysalis, in which it will transform into an adult.

Tortoiseshell butterfly caterpillars live in a group for the first few weeks of their lives.

Attached to a leaf or a stem, the chrysalis changes color as the days go by.

After about two weeks in the chrysalis, the butterfly emerges. It has the form of an adult with wings that are very colorful!

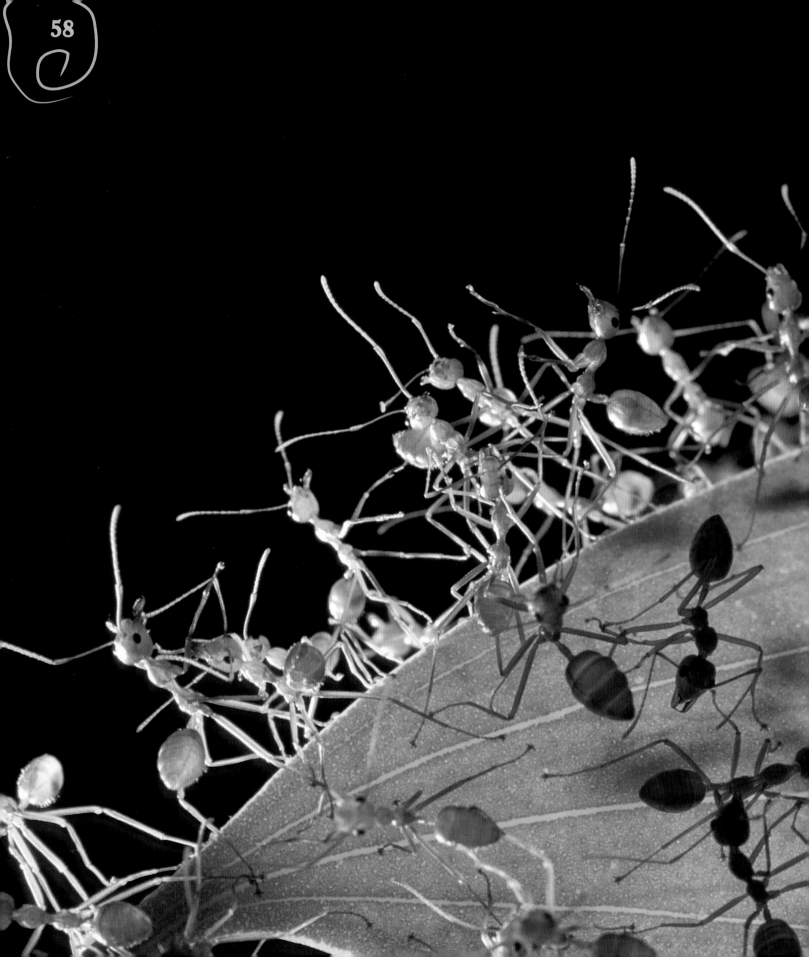

Social Lives

Insects do not speak, but they do communicate... sometimes in surprising ways. Insects like bees, ants, and termites even live together.

Communicating

Insects have several means of communication.
They use all of their five senses to exchange information.

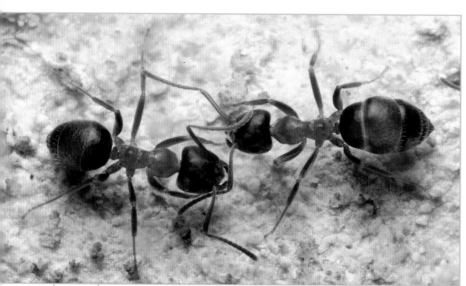

What are these ants "saying"
to each other?

An Ant's World

If you watch ants scurrying around, you will notice that individuals often touch each others' antennae. This means of communication is often accompanied by exchanging food directly from one mouth to the other. This is called trophallaxis.

Singing

Insects do not use their mouths to sing.
They emit sounds from other parts of their bodies.
A grasshopper rubs two bodies parts together to form music. It may rub a leg against the body or against a wing or rub two wings together.

The cicada makes music using organs
on its abdomen called tymbals.

Thanks to his comb-like antennae, the male cream-spot tiger can pick up a female's scent from far away.

A Great Sense of Smell

Communication between insects often happens by exchanging scents called pheromones. Insects do not have noses. They use their antennae to pick up the scents of others.

A Flashlight

Certain species of firefly and glow worms produce a small greenish light that you can see on summer nights. This light is said to be cold—meaning that it does not get warm like a fire or a lightbulb.

Although it may look like one, a glow worm is not a worm. It is an insect.

A Termite Nest

Termites live in groups called colonies. They build nests underground and in buildings. The largest nests can be 33 feet (10 meters) tall.

Long Live the Queen

After mating, the queen lays eggs for the rest of her life. In some species the queen lays thousands of eggs every day. Queens can live up to 25 years.

Look at how big the queen is compared to the other members of the colony.

Inside the Colony

In addition to the king and queen, the colony includes soldiers and worker termites. Soldiers defend the nest. Workers maintain the nest and feed and care for the young.

In some species, soldier termites have large mandibles. In others, they shoot defensive chemicals.

An Air-Conditioned House

The termite nest is made of earth that has been chewed and then hardened by the sun. It is very solid. The walls let some air come in so the temperature remains the same, even if it is very warm outside. Just like in a house, the termite nest has several bedrooms connected by hallways.

In Africa and Australia, termite nests are big, tall, and imposing. Some people call them cathedrals.

An Anthill

Ants are very social animals that live in a very structured community. Many species live in anthills.

A Shelter Full of Life

Whether it is easily visible or hidden underground, the anthill is always made up of numerous galleries that connect all the chambers. Some of these rooms house the eggs or larvae; others are used as storerooms.

In the woods, red ants use debris from plants to construct an anthill in the shape of a dome.

Flying Ants

In the spring, males and females from different anthills fly away together. It is a nuptial flight. The females that mate will lay eggs and start a new anthill. When that happens, they will lose their wings.

Once a year, you can see ants with wings. They are getting ready to reproduce.

The Brood

The queen entrusts her eggs to specialized workers.
During the day they move the eggs to the top of
the anthill, where they will be warm.
At night, they move them back down.

Sorting and transporting eggs,
larvae, and nymphs is a daily job
for the brood workers.

A Hidden Queen

Once moved in, the queen remains in the anthill
to lay eggs. It is therefore very difficult to see her.
And you shouldn't go looking! If you touch an
anthill you will upset the thousands of soldier
ants whose job it is to protect the queen.

The queen is the largest ant in the colony.

A Beehive

A colony of bees is made up of a queen, up to 80,000 worker bees, and up to 800 males called drones. There are also thousands of eggs and immature bees.

A Swarm of Bees

In the wild, a bee's nest is built in a natural hive, like a hollow tree, for example. Bees may also live in a hive made by people. In spring, if there are too many bees, half of the colony leaves with the queen. They move off in a swarm to populate a new hive that scout bees have already located.

A swarm will stop and cluster on a tree before flying to its new home.

The Bee's Dance

When a bee finds a source of food, she indicates the direction and the distance to the other workers by performing what's known as a waggle dance. The bee moves around in a figure-eight pattern and flutters her wings. This tells the other bees exactly where to go!

Bees cannot speak like you. They communicate with each other by dancing!

The queen is recognizable by her long abdomen. She is always surrounded by worker bees who feed her.

It's Good to Be the Queen!

All of the workers are sisters because they have the same mother—the queen. The queen lives several years while the workers live only about 40 days.

Offense
and
Defense

Stinging, biting, tricking, hiding...
Insects use formidable weapons and
other surprising tricks to defend
themselves or to attack.

That Hurts!

Some insects sting in order to kill prey for food or to defend themselves. They can inject a very powerful venom that can even be dangerous for people.

Venom

Venom is a poison made by certain animals. It is used in self defense, or to immobilize or kill prey.

Some scorpions use venom to immobilize their prey.

The Stinger

To inject the venom, insects need a fine needle, called a stinger. It is located at the end of the abdomen. If a honeybee stings you it will die, because it cannot pull its stinger back out of your skin. Other bees don't have the same problem!

The wasp does not hesitate to sting several times in a row when it feels threatened.

Paralyzing

The female red-banded sand wasp paralyzes a caterpillar without killing it and then transports it to her nest. An egg is laid directly in the body of the victim. The larva will then devour the caterpillar.

The female red-banded sand wasp paralzyes a caterpillar with several stings.

Sucking

In some insects, like the horse fly, the mouthpart is called a rostrum. It is sort of like a syringe. Females use the rostrum to prick an animal's skin and drink its blood. These insects fly silently, so they can land on their victims without them even noticing.

The female horse fly uses its rostrum to suck blood rather than inject venom.

Piercing and Sucking

The assassin bug is so named because it grabs its prey and holds it still while repeatedly stabbing it to death. The assassin then injects a toxin into its prey. The animal's tissues dissolve and are sucked out by the assassin bug.

The assassin bug is known as a piercing-sucking insect because it pierces its victim before sucking out its insides.

A Deep Bite

Predators are species that feed on other animals. In the world of bugs and insects, they use their mandibles like daggers!

A Killer Punch

The front legs of a praying mantis form very effective pincers that help it catch insects before biting them. The pincers jump out like a spring as soon as an insect passes by. It is impossible to escape once the prey is caught in this trap!

A praying mantis can catch and eat everything from insects to small birds!

Venom-Filled Fangs

The bite of an insect goes from painful to lethal if the bite is accompanied by venom.

The scolopendra uses fangs called forcipules to bite its prey and inject it with poison.

The assassin fly (right) can capture a dragonfly in full flight.

Death in Mid-Flight

Assassin flies hunt while flying. The fly grabs its prey with its legs and then bites it in the back or side. Then the assassin injects its prey with venomous saliva. The prey dies instantly. The venom also liquefies the prey's insides.

Mandibles

Predatory insects often have well-defined mandibles. They can kill prey in different ways. Long mandibles are good for piercing and strong mandibles are used for cutting and crushing.

The green tiger beetle uses its long mandibles to catch caterpillars.

Tricky Spiders

Not all spiders weave webs to catch prey. Some create elaborate traps. Others just lie in wait and then pounce!

Trapdoor spiders are not aggressive— toward humans anyway!

Trapdoor Spiders

This spider is named for the inventive way in which it catches prey. The trapdoor builds a burrow underground that is lined with silk and covered with a trapdoor made of soil and vegetation. When the spider feels the vibration of passing prey, it leaps out and grabs it!

If a trapdoor spider is threatened it may show its fangs in self-defense.

The Gooty sapphire ornamental tree spider
lives in trees. It prefers to eat flying insects,
but can take down prey as large as a mouse.

Bluffing

Many animals come up with creative ways to get out of a fight.

Nobody Move!

As danger approaches, some insects play dead. They stay very still and often tuck up their legs. They don't even hesitate to let themselves fall from several inches in order to disappear among the plants.

This coleoptera really seems to be dead... but it is only waiting for danger to pass!

Warning Colors

Many brightly colored animals are advertising that they are poisonous or taste bad. Predators know to leave them alone. Some insects specialize in mimicking the colors of these animals—even though they neither taste bad nor are unsafe to eat!

This fly's yellow-and-black coloring makes it look like a wasp.

The blood-spewing beetle spits a small droplet of reddish liquid when threatened.

Spitting

Some insects secrete a foul-tasting liquid to defend themselves against birds. The liquid may be secreted from their mouths or from joints in their legs.

The owl butterfly has two eye spots on its wings. These may serve to scare predators away.

Illusionists

Some species have colors or designs on their wings that offer protection. Some designs may startle or frighten predators. Others may make the insect look like something unappetizing—like bird droppings, for example.

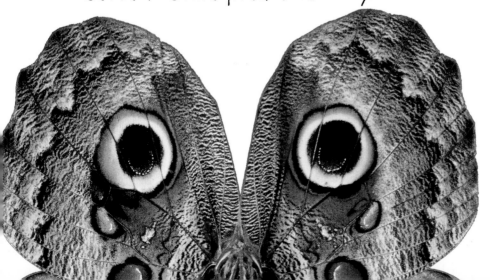

Hide and Seek

Going unnoticed is often the best self-defense for many insects. In some species, their shape and colors can make them almost invisible.

Walking Sticks

A walking stick has the shape and coloring of a twig or small branch. It is easily camouflaged among plants. And if danger approaches, it knows how to remain perfectly still.

Can you find the walking stick among these grasses?

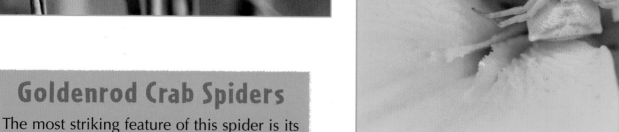

Goldenrod Crab Spiders

The most striking feature of this spider is its ability to change from white to yellow to blend in with its surroundings. This type of camouflage is called homochromy.

Where is the spider?

Peppered Moths

The peppered moth spends its days on a tree trunk...but not the trunk of just any tree! The moth always chooses the silver birch because its wings blend in almost perfectly with the trunk.

Look carefully at the tree bark. There is a peppered moth hiding on it.

Leaf Insects

In the middle of the forest, insects that look like leaves are difficult to find. The true leaf insect goes even further. Its movements are abrupt, making it look like a leaf blowing in the wind.

Another name for this true leaf insect is walking leaf.

Leafhoppers

The leafhopper is an insect that lives in the trees. It imitates plants with its shape and color. This incredible disguise does not always trick its enemies, however.

The leafhopper looks exactly like a real leaf... with all of its imperfections!

Super Structures

Everything is potential building material when it comes to making shelters: earth, pebbles, silk, plant remnants... and even paper!

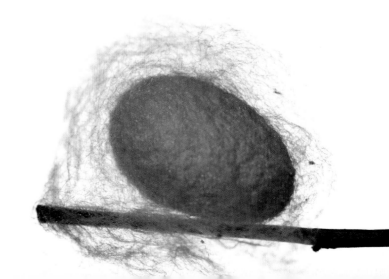

Masonry

Wet earth is very practical for making a hiding place or nest. The structures may be built to shelter larvae or to serve as food storage units.

Black-and-Yellow Mud Daubers

The black-and-yellow mud dauber is a solitary hunting wasp that is also a great builder. The female makes a nest made of up mud cells, which she fills with paralyzed spiders to feed her larvae.

The black-and-yellow mud dauber rolls small balls of fresh wet clay earth to make her nest.

Red Mason Bees

The red mason bee looks for natural small holes in hollow plant stems, cliffsides, and old buildings. The female lines each cell of the nest with mud and pollen. The insect's work is as perfect and as clean as a true mason's!

The red mason is a small solitary bee. Each cell in her nest contains a larva and food reserves.

The sweat bee's nest is a hole in the ground. Its entrance is a round hole surrounded by fragments of earth.

The Sweat Bee's Well

The sweat bee digs a vertical well 8 to 11 inches (20 to 28 centimeters) deep in earth that has been hardened by the sun. Often, several sweat bees will live next to each other.

Paper-Mâché

Insects were capable of making paper well before humans...
even though they can't write or draw!

Wasps make nests to house their larvae—one to each cell.

A Paper Nest

Many species of wasps and hornets use a paper-mâché like substance to make their nests. They gather dead wood from trees and mix it with their saliva. They create the nest a little at a time, adding new cells as the colony gets bigger.

This European paper wasp chews on a piece of wood to make paper.

The paper made by wasps and
hornets is not pure white like
the paper you draw on.
That's because it's made from a
variety of woods.

Miners

One of the safest places to make a home is in the ground.
Insects use every tool at their disposal to dig—
mouth, head, and legs.

Great Golden Digger Wasps

The female great golden digger wasp digs a deep tunnel that branches out at the end. She lays a single egg in each branch and stores prey there for when the larvae hatch.

The great golden digger uses the spiny brushes on her legs to dig a burrow for a nest.

Red-Banded Sand Wasps

The female red-banded sand wasp digs her burrow in the ground. It's a hallway a few inches long that leads to a room where she puts her prey—usually caterpillars.

The red-banded sand wasp uses its powerful mandibles to pull gravel from its burrow.

The trench digging beetle uses its flat head and front legs to dig.

Trench Digging Beetles

This beetle has found a clever way to live in the dry deserts of Namibia. It digs a trench in the side of a sand dune. As tiny water droplets condense on the walls of the trench, the beetle licks them up.

Mole Crickets

Mole crickets burrow down beneath the grass. They create tunnels for moving from place to place. Females make their nests and lay their eggs underground.

The European mole cricket has large front legs. It uses them like shovels to dig.

Weavers

A lot of insects and spiders know how to make and weave threads of silk. They may be thin or thick, dry or sticky.

Silk Makers

Both caterpillars and spiders have spinnerets for making silk. A caterpillar's spinneret is on its head; the spider's is on its abdomen.

When the garden spider catches prey, it quickly rolls it in silk. The spider will eat it later...

Sewing a Nest

Weaver ants work together to built their nests in trees. They sew leaves together using silk produced by their larvae.

The weaver ant carries a larva in its mouth and moves it over the spaces to be joined.

A Downy Nest

Pine processionary caterpillars move by making a single file line. In winter, they weave a silky nest where they spend the days. At night, they come out to eat pine needles.

Pine processionary caterpillars destroy the trees in which they nest.

An Isolated Cocoon

A moth caterpillar transforms into a pupa toward the end of its metamorphosis. Many species create a cocoon out of silk. The pupa will remain inside until it emerges as a winged adult moth.

The cocoon hardens as it dries to form a solid enclosure.

A Community Cocoon

Bird-cherry ermine moth caterpillars form community silk shelters. They weave together a large web that covers entire branches of bushes. They then eat all the leaves.

Wrapped in a dense network of silk, bird-cherry ermine moth pupae are protected from predators.

Spider Webs

Spider webs are efficient traps for catching insects. Though they are all made of silk, webs come in a variety of shapes.

Orb Weavers

Orb weaver webs are made of concentric circles (smaller circles inside larger ones) connected by spokes. Their silk strands are sticky and catch insects in mid-flight. Some species stay in the middle of their web while others hide to wait for their prey.

When a web is ruined, the spider eats the silk to make a new one. That's a nice job of recycling...

Dome Webs

Some spiders make their webs in the shape of a dome, then they hide underneath. When an insect lands on top, the spider makes a hole in the web to grab its prey.

Numerous threads secure this small silk dome to the plants above and below it.

Some webs are built horizontally and lay like a sheet over plants and shrubs. They can cover large areas.

Sheet Webs

Sheet web spiders weave horizontal webs that they hang beneath. Above the sheet are strands of web meant to knock flying insects down onto the sheet. The spider then bites through the web to paralyze its prey.

Funnel Webs

Some spiders build funnel-shaped webs. The webs usually have a flat surface for catching prey and a funnel-like tube where the spider hides. Once the prey is stuck in its web, the spider scurries up to grab it.

The barn funnel weaver can be found in barns and in homes.

All Dressed Up!

With some debris and a little silk, the larvae of some insects make themselves fancy covers called sheaths.

Sheaths

The larvae of moths from the psychida family construct elaborate cases around themselves that are known as sheaths. These are made from plant debris and other natural materials found nearby.
The larvae of caddisflies do the same. These are aquatic insects, so their sheaths would be made of materials found in or near the water.

This caddisfly larva made a beautiful sheath with lots of colorful pebbles that she found in a river.

The caddisfly larva also uses little pieces of wood, grass, and leaves to build its sheath.

Only the head and thorax of the bagworm moth extend outside its sheath. This enables it to move around and feed on nearby plants.

We Recycle!

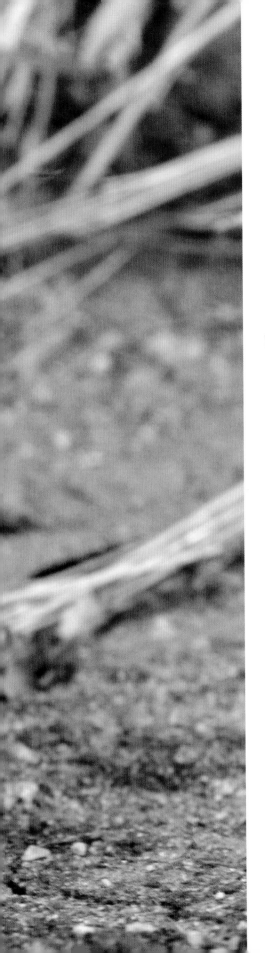

Insects called saprophages are nature's cleaning crew.
They eat decomposing plants, dead animals, and even excrement.

Dead Wood

Without dead wood eaters it would take a very long time for trees to decompose. That, in turn, would delay the growth of new trees.

Hard Wood

Larvae of some types of longhorn beetles and coleoptera are capable of digesting dead wood that is still hard. As they eat it, they dig holes and galleries, making the wood look like Swiss cheese!

The longhorn beetle larva looks like a fat white worm. It leaves a trail of sawdust as it bores through the wood.

Rotten Wood

In general, insects like the European rhinoceros beetle prefer wood that has been dead a long time because it is already rotten and soft. The female looks for dead trees as a place to lay her eggs.

The European rhinoceros beetle is named for the long horn on the male's head.

Under the Bark

Some insects and bugs, including the clown beetle, hunt other insects that live in dead wood. These predators live beneath the bark of the dead tree.

Both adult and larval clown beetles are dead-wood-dwelling insects.

In Holes

Hermit beetles live in tree hollows that contain loose dead wood. Females lay their eggs in the hollow and the larvae survive by eating the rotten wood. A hermit beetle's entire lifecycle can take place within the hollow of the tree in which it was born.

Some people think hermit beetles smell like peaches or plums!

In the Trunk

The wood wasp is a large wasp that lays its eggs in the wood of dead or decaying trees. The female uses her long ovipositor to drill into the wood and then she lays one to seven eggs. Larvae can spend up to five years in a tree trunk.

The long appendage on the female wood wasp is not a stinger. It is an ovipositor.

Animal Remains

Animals that feed on the flesh of dead animals are not put off by the smell of decomposing bodies. In fact, it helps them find their food!

Scavengers

Several creatures, like beetles, fly larvae, ants, and wasps, are carrion feeders. The different species colonize the carcass at different times. When they leave the body another species arrives.

Some insects, like flies, lay their eggs in the bodies of dead animals.

The Finishers

Skin, hair, and feathers are not easy to digest. But coleoptera of the dermestes family love them! They sometimes invade museums because they find food there: animals stuffed for collections, and different kinds of debris...

This little dermestes is called a carpet beetle. It also eats things made from animal skins, like rugs, fur coats, and leather clothes.

The crayfish uses its large pincers to cut up dead fish and eat them.

Crayfish

Crayfish are found in freshwater. They are omnivores, which means they eat everything— plants, fish, insects, and even dead animals as long as they are relatively fresh.

Dead Plants

Dead leaves that fall in autumn make a carpet.
This bedding is eaten by insects that often go unnoticed.

Eating

The ground is like a huge buffet for creatures in the area. Animals like springtails, earthworms, and millipedes feed on the leaf litter, breaking it up into little pieces. Then other animals come along to eat the smaller pieces.

Springtails live in the leaf litter. They eat fungi, algae, and other plant materials.

Collecting Crumbs

The silverfish is an insect with small silvery scales that mostly lives in forests, in warm and humid places. It eats tiny debris left by other insects that were eating dead plants.

Silverfish are sometimes found inside houses, too.

Millipedes live in the upper layer of leaf litter where it is moist.

Transformers

Millipedes come out at night to eat decaying plants, moss, and fungi. By digesting them, the millipedes transform them into compost that will be used to nourish plants.

An earthworm can eat up to one-third of its body weight in one day!

Burrowing

Earthworms eat through decaying leaves and roots as they tunnel through the soil. As they move along, these nutrients are transported through their excrement. In this way, they keep the soil healthy.

Poop

Coprophagous insects eat the dung of other animals. You can see some moving around on the excrement, but there are others hidden inside.

This dung is entirely covered with flies that have come to mate and lay eggs in it.

Flies

Adult flies eat poop. They also lay their eggs in it. The eggs hatch within 24 hours and then the larvae emerge. They feed on the dung for about five days before leaving to find a dry dark place in which to pupate.

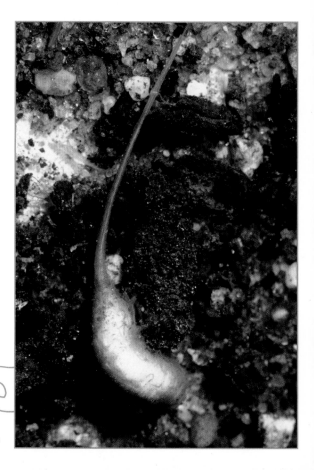

Droneflies

The dronefly is a fly with yellow and black stripes. Its larvae have a unique shape that is the reason for their nickname: rat-tailed maggots. They live in stagnant water or liquid excrement.

Dronefly larvae are able to breathe through the excrement thanks to a long tube that they use like a snorkel.

Most dung beetles prefer the poop of herbivores.

Dung Beetles

Dung beetle larvae eat solid dung to extract undigested nutritients from it. Adult dung beetles suck the moisture out of dung.

Naughty or Nice?

Insects have an important role in nature. For example, some help humans grow plants. But others can be dangerous.

In the Forest

There are insects that destroy trees in some forests. But other insects are really useful! They need to be protected.

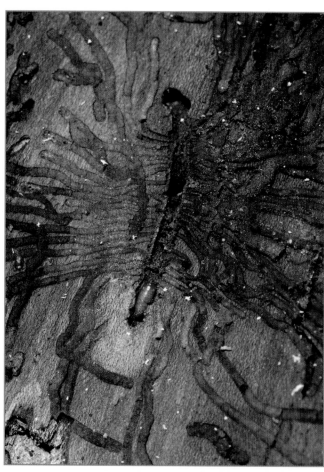

Bark Beetles

Bark beetles feed on the inner bark of trees. That causes the flow of nutrients from the leaves to the rest of the tree to be cut off. One bark beetle alone can't cause much damage. But when trees become infested, whole forests can come under threat.

The bark beetle's network of galleries makes beautiful designs under the bark.

Caterpillar Hunters

This beetle was introduced in North America to reduce the number of gypsy moths. Gypsy moths destroy forests by eating leaves. Caterpillar hunters save many trees by eating huge numbers of gypsy moths and their larvae.

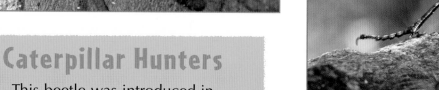

Adult caterpillar hunters climb trees to catch their prey.

The gypsy moth caterpillar is the number one most destructive insect for forests. It is very hairy and has blue and red excrescences.

Gypsy Moths

In some years, gypsy moths reproduce at an alarming rate. Then all the trees in the area are in danger. The gypsy moth caterpillars can eat huge amounts of leaves.

Rosalia Longicorn

An insect of remarkable beauty, the rosalia longicorn is threatened with extinction. It lives in the dead wood of old beech tree forests, which are rapidly disappearing from the Earth. Rosalia longicorn is protected in several countries.

The longicorn's lifecycle from egg to adult takes at least three years.

Pollination

Insects that fly from flower to flower to eat carry pollen on their bodies. This is pollination. Without these visitors, there would be no fruit and no new flowers!

Removal

The yellow powder produced by flowers is called pollen. It is the seed of the male plant. When insects like bees, butterflies, and coleoptera come to eat the flowers' nectar or pollen, they quickly end up covered in tiny grains of pollen.

The yellow grains covering this wasp beetle are pollen.

Transportation

One flower is not enough to feed an insect. It has to visit several dozen, even hundreds, each day. Each time the insect lands, grains of pollen come off its hairs and others stick to them. This is how flowers reproduce.

Some grains of pollen that this bee gathered from another flower fall onto this flower.

More than 100 crops in the United States depend on honeybees for pollination.

Professional Pollinators

Honeybees are very useful because they help pollinate many plants farmed by people. Farmers build beehives in their orchards to be sure that they will have fruit and vegetables.

Garden Helpers

Certain species help in the garden by eating other insects that attack plants.

Glowworms

Adult glowworms and their larvae eat snails and slugs. These are two notorious plant eaters!

Glowworms work together to finish off a big snail.

Predatory Stink Bugs

Some stink bugs eat only destructive insects, such as plant-eating bugs, beetles, and caterpillars. They serve as a natural insecticide. In this way, they protect vegetable plants and fruit trees.

The predatory stink bug attacks larvae from harmful insects.

Beetles use their strong jaws to chew their food.

Ground Beetles

These beetles eat slugs, maggots, snails, and other garden pests. Just one larva can make a difference in the garden. It can eat more than 50 caterpillars.

Green Lacewings

Green lacewing larvae are sometimes called aphid lions because they eat so many of these small plant-destroying insects.

Adult lacewings are also pollinators.

Ladybugs

Ladybugs are a gardener's best friend. This species protects crops and plants by eating destructive insects.

A ladybug lays her eggs on a plant that has been infested with aphids. When the larvae hatch they eat aphids by the hundreds.

An Efficient Predator

Both adult ladybugs and their larvae eat aphids and mealybugs. Both types of bugs can kill a plant by sucking out its sap. That is why ladybugs are raised to be released in great numbers on farms.

The ladybug nymph remains immobile in a chrysalis attached to a leaf. It does not eat. All of its energy is spent transforming into an adult.

To recognize the seven-spotted ladybug, you just have to count the dots on its red elytra. There are seven: no more, no less.

Destroyers

Some insects eat crops.
In large numbers they can cause a lot of damage.

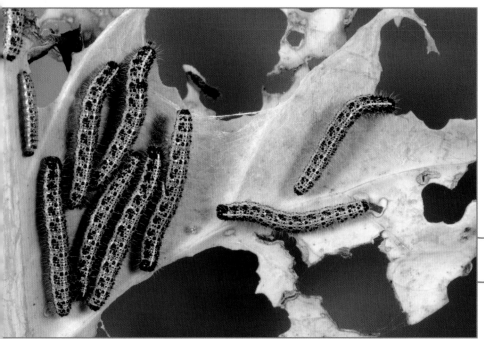

Cabbage Butterflies

The cabbage butterfly is beautiful but destructive. The female lays her eggs on the undersides of plants that her caterpillars like to eat, like cabbage.

Cabbage butterfly caterpillars can destroy whole cabbage fields.

Migratory Locusts

Swarms of migratory locusts can contain millions of individuals. When this cloud of insects pours down on a field, there is nothing left at all after just a few hours.

Migratory locusts may often go unnoticed... until they begin to swarm.

A female potato beetle lays between 300 and 800 eggs.

Colorado Potato Beetles

This yellow and black pest devours potato plants in both its larval and adult forms. They are found in many places around the world—not just Colorado!

Garden Slugs

Roots, stems, leaves—nothing escapes a slug's appetite. When slugs attack very young plants, they can eat the whole thing entirely. They eat different kinds of vegetables including lettuce, potatoes, and other plants.

Slugs eat up to 40% of their body weight every day. What a disaster for the vegetable garden!

Undesirables

Many bothersome insects can be found around the world. They attack people or the environment.

Asian Predatory Wasps

Asian predatory wasps prey on honeybees and other insects. They will even attack humans in defense of their nests.

The Asian predatory wasp has more black than yellow on its body.

Clothes Moths

The larvae of the clothes moth think wool from sweaters is a delicious treat.
They quietly slip into the back of closets, eat the clothing fibers, and make little holes.
They can also cause of lot of damage to clothes made of cotton or silk, and even rugs.

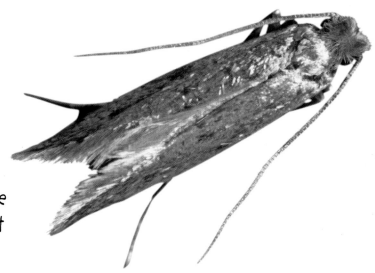

Adult clothes moths won't give you any trouble. But watch out for their larvae!

The cockroach finds its food, like this sugar cube, in garbage cans and kitchen cabinets. It runs and hides at the slightest sign of danger.

Cockroaches

Cockroaches live among humans. They love warm buildings and wait for night to come out to eat. Cockroaches can spread sickness— and are very hard to get rid of.

Body Lice

The body louse is tiny—about the size of a sesame seed. Lice attach to the scalp to suck blood, which causes the head to become very itchy. A louse's white eggs, called nits, attach to the base of individual hairs. You have to look very carefully to find them.

The body louse travels by moving from head to head. It does not fly.

Disease Carriers

Some insects can transmit diseases when they bite.
Luckily there are vaccines to protect us.

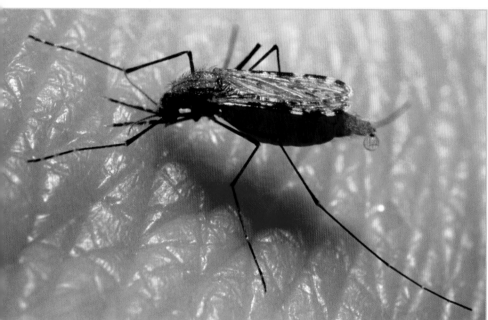

Mosquitoes

Some mosquitoes carry a variety of infectious diseases, including malaria, dengue, Zika, and West Nile virus. More than one million people around the world die from mosquito-borne illnesses every year.

As a mosquito moves from host to host, it spreads any infection it might be carrying.

Ticks

Animals are commonly plagued by ticks. They attach themselves to the animals' skin and suck their blood. They can also attack people. Deer ticks are a particular problem for humans. They carry Lyme disease.

After you play outside, be sure to check yourself carefully. A tick might have hitched a ride on your clothes.

The assassin bug is an ambush predator.

Milkweed Assassin Bugs

The bite of an assassin bug is very painful. And, in Central and South America, it can be deadly. In those regions, some assassins transmit a deadly illness called Chagas disease.

Tsetse flies attack humans and animals.

Tsetse Flies

Tsetse flies are found in sub-Saharan Africa. This fly has a painful bite, and it can also transmit what is known as sleeping sickness. Left untreated, the disease can cause death.

Yummy Honey

Have you ever tasted honey? Did you know that it is made by bees and collected by a beekeeper?

Beekeeping

Raising bees is called beekeeping or apiculture. In nature, bees live in a group and take shelter in the trunk of a hollow tree. When they are raised by beekeepers, they live in manufactured hives.

Bees collect nectar from flowers to make honey. They also gather pollen that they store on their legs.

Inside the hive are many small cells. They contain honey or bee larvae.

The beekeeper has to stay protected to avoid getting stung.

Insects you can Eat

Insects have been a great source of protein for people around the world for many years.

For Sale

It is possible to find insects ready to eat in open-air markets around the world. They are especially popular in places like Mexico, Ghana, China, Japan, and Thailand.

In markets in China, you can buy skewers of cicada and scorpion larvae.

A Lot of Choices

Around the world, more than 2,000 species of insects are eaten. The most abundant and the easiest ones to catch are the ones that are eaten the most. Others, more rare ones, are sought after because of their special taste or because they taste sugary, like candy.

Some people say silkworm chrysalises are delicious!

Insects can be grilled on skewers—just like a chicken kebab!

Various Recipes

Raw, grilled, boiled, dried, smoked, plain or with a sauce; there are many different ways to cook insects. Some people like to toast roaches to make them good and crunchy. Others spread worms on toast like butter.

All Over the World

Insects are eaten by people in more than 100 countries, mostly in Africa, Asia, and Central America. You can also taste them in Europe and the United States. You can find them in specialty stores or certain restaurants.

This child is enjoying a stick insect.

Index

Photo Credits